HOW TO LEAD A LIFEBUILDER STUDY

JACK KUHATSCHEK & CINDY BUNCH

9 STUDIES
FOR INDIVIDUALS
OR GROUPS

Life
Builder
Study

INTER-VARSITY PRESS
36 Causton Street, London SW1P 4ST, England
Email: ivp@ivpbooks.com
Website: www.ivpbooks.com

Originally published in the United States of America in 1967 by InterVarsity Press, Downers Grove, Illinois, as Leading Bible Discussions *by James F. Nyquist*
Second edition published in 1985 as Leading Bible Discussions *by James F. Nyquist and Jack Kuhatschek*
Third edition published in 2003 as How to Lead a LifeGuide Bible Study *by Jack Kuhatschek and Cindy Bunch*
First published in Great Britain in 2018

British Library Cataloguing-in-Publication Data
A catalogue record for this book is available from the British Library.

ISBN: 978-1-78359-686-7
eBook ISBN: 978-1-78359-687-4

Printed in Great Britain by Ashford Colour Press Ltd, Gosport, Hampshire

Inter-Varsity Press publishes Christian books that are true to the Bible and that communicate the gospel, develop discipleship and strengthen the church for its mission in the world.

IVP originated within the Inter-Varsity Fellowship, now the Universities and Colleges Christian Fellowship, a student movement connecting Christian Unions in universities and colleges throughout Great Britain, and a member movement of the International Fellowship of Evangelical Students. Website: www.uccf.org.uk. That historic association is maintained, and all senior IVP staff and committee members subscribe to the UCCF Basis of Faith.

Contents

Preface

This is the third (US but first UK) edition of a handbook—a product of InterVarsity back in its early days—that has been an important tool for church, dorm and neighborhood groups both within InterVarsity and far beyond, with over 200,000 copies in circulation.

The original *Leading Bible Discussions* was written by James F. Nyquist in 1967 as a revision of his booklet *Conducting Bible Studies*, published in the 1950s. The long-standing nature of the principles outlined decades ago reinforces the truism "There are no new ideas, just new ways to edit."

Continuing to shine through the book are the sound inductive Bible study principles developed in InterVarsity Christian Fellowship by Bible teachers who influenced Jim Nyquist—people like Jane Hollingsworth Haile, Dorothy Farmer and Barbara Boyd (all building on the teaching of Robert Traina). My own understanding of Scripture was transformed when I learned how to study inductively during my college years in the Blue Ridge region of InterVarsity, where small groups are the centerpiece of regional director Jimmy Long's ministry. I have received help in understanding how to recontexualize these ideas for the current generation from InterVarsity's current Bible Study Task Force, especially from Bob Grahmann and Curtis Chang.

In the 1980s, along with other InterVarsity Press editors such as Jim Hoover and Andy Le Peau, Jack Kuhatschek created the LifeGuide® Bible Study line (the LifeBuilder series in the UK), launched in 1985.

Jack rewrote *Leading Bible Discussions* to be a companion volume for the new series, adding new material about how to lead a group with a guide and illustrations from small group life. Jack is one of the finest Bible study writers I know. If you look through IVP's list of titles, you will find a number of guides that he has written.

In 1990 I began editing LifeBuilder guides. Then in 1995 I put together a plan (now nearly complete) to revise and update the series. I have done a corresponding revision in this book to fit the principles to the current series format, so that you can lead the best study possible.

Enjoy!

Cindy Bunch
Senior Editor, InterVarsity Press

1

The Power
of a Small Group

My* first small group experience was in my freshman year of college. I was plunged into a web of complex relationships. I developed a crush on the leader—who was secretly dating the coleader—and I had a personality conflict with one of the group members. But in the midst of all that emotion, I remained committed to the weekly meetings. As the weeks passed, the crush faded and, better yet, the personality conflict turned into a lasting friendship. Best of all, I discovered that I loved talking about the Bible and praying with others. Ever since, small groups have been an essential part of my spiritual growth.

I've been in lots of kinds of groups: book discussion, writing and arts, recovery, even church committees. But I find I get the most out of the groups that focus on the Bible. It's the process of opening the Scripture as equals and drawing out the meaning together that stimulates me. I find that listening to others talk about how they live out these passages helps me enormously in applying the Bible to my own life.

What Does a Bible Discussion Look Like?
In a good group Bible study there's lots of interaction. The leader is not a teacher or "answer person." Everyone contributes ideas.

---

* "My" and "I" refer to Cindy Bunch throughout this book (see preface).

Here's how Jack Kuhatschek, the first editor of the LifeBuilders, describes what happens in a typical Bible study session.

The study had already begun when we arrived. People were seated in a circle with Bibles in their laps. At first it was difficult to tell who was leading. Conversation crisscrossed from person to person. Everyone seemed to be involved.

The study that day was on the book of Jonah. We took our seats and were quickly caught up in the discussion. It was Darcy's turn to be leading, so she spoke up and said, "God told Jonah to go preach to the pagan city of Nineveh, but Jonah headed off in the opposite direction. How did God respond to his disobedience?"

We all looked down at our Bibles for a moment, then Steve said, "God judged Jonah for disobeying him." He explained that poor Jonah had nearly been shipwrecked, was thrown overboard, was swallowed by a large fish, spent three days and nights in its stomach and then was vomited on dry land.

Sandy agreed with Steve but felt that God was also merciful to Jonah. "After all," she said, "he could have let Jonah drown. Or he might have let him stay in the belly of the fish until he had been digested!"

After the laughter, there was a brief pause. "Anything else?" Darcy asked.

Curtis, who had been quiet up to that point, decided to join in. "God knew what it would take to bring Jonah to repentance. By the time he was back safely on dry land, and the word of the Lord came to him a second time, Jonah was more than willing to consider going to Nineveh!"

We went on like this for about forty-five minutes. Periodically Darcy would ask another question from our study guide. ("What was Jonah's reaction to the destruction of the plant?" "How does God's attitude toward the people of Nineveh compare with Jonah's?") Then several of us would respond, being careful to base our answers on the text before us.

Our Wednesday night group consists of a computer programmer, a homemaker, a marketing specialist, a publicist, an InterVarsity staff member, an editor and an artist. Darcy is a part-time secretary. None of us is ordained; only one person is involved in "full-time Christian work." Yet it was amazing how much we learned from each other. Each person provided a unique perspective on this brief but challenging book of the Bible. Together we relived Jonah's experiences. We felt sorry for him. We were amused at him. Most importantly, we identified with him!

We also got a fresh look at God, especially his care for people— even those we disapprove of. He lovingly disciplined Jonah. He had compassion on the people of Nineveh, even though they were part of a ruthless, idolatrous nation. His justice and judgment were unmistakable. But they were overshadowed by his mercy, love and forgiveness.

By the end of the discussion we were exhausted, but we had been stimulated, instructed and encouraged.

What Makes It Work?

If you are the leader, then I have some great news for you: What makes a LifeBuilder Bible Study so exciting for the group members is that the leader stays in the background. You don't have to be a gifted communicator or a biblical studies major to lead one of these discussions. All you need are some well-written questions and some basic communication skills to help people open up. The questions will encourage group members to dig into the text for their responses and the application will flow naturally out of their own lives.

This type of study also has a number of benefits.

1. *People learn how to feed themselves from the Scriptures.* Each member of the group is involved in discovering the meaning of the passage. For some, this kind of involvement is a new experience. They are used to being told what the Scriptures say. They may know a lot about the Bible, but what they know is the result of someone else's

study, not their own. A Bible discussion encourages them to search the Scriptures for themselves. For many, the Bible comes alive in a way they have never experienced before.

2. *It encourages regular patterns of Bible study.* A Bible discussion provides an opportunity for regular personal Bible study in a small group, which may help people carve out study disciplines on their own as well.

3. *Everyone has an opportunity to participate.* Because the group is small (eight to ten people is best), the very nature of the group encourages members to be involved. They begin to realize that their contributions are crucial to the learning experience. Even people who might never have spoken up in a large group begin to open up.

4. *We benefit from other people's insights.* As each person shares, all of us gain a fuller understanding of a passage and how it applies to our lives.

5. *Participants become part of a caring community.* A group study provides a natural setting in which to get to know one another and to cultivate honest, open relationships. The members of the group pray for each other and care for each other in practical ways.

6. *The leader learns from the group members.* It isn't necessary for you to know more about the passage than anyone else. In fact, there may be times when you will ask the group a question that you cannot answer. But you will look into the passage and uncover the meaning together.

How Do I Go About Leading?

If you've been in a small group before, you may have had some negative experiences. For example, have you ever been in a Bible study where the leader sat down and just started reading through the questions—and you could tell that was the first time the leader had opened the guide? Have you ever been in a group where people spent the whole time talking about television or sports—and never got to the Bible? Have you ever been in a group where one group member did all the talking? We want to help you navigate these dangerous small group waters.

Leading a Bible discussion is not difficult, but it does require some skills. This book is designed to provide you with those skills by walking you through each component of a LifeBuilder Bible Study and describing how to use it. So we begin at the beginning—what to study.

2

Choosing a
Bible Study Guide

You will probably want to begin your small group with dinner or an informal social gathering. During your first meeting, try to discover people's interests and needs. Begin by asking whether they would prefer to study a biblical book, character or topic.

Beware of being swayed by one individual's pet peeves or pet topics. Select a study topic and format that will meet the needs and interests of the majority. And if a topic is too complex and out of your depth, don't be afraid to admit it. I find that whenever I ask a group what they want to study, the answer that comes back is Revelation. That is an exciting book to study together but may not be the best starting place for a group! Request that you begin with a simpler study.

During the first meeting, you may wish to ask how the Bible has helped the people in the group. As they describe their own history with the Bible, group members will have a chance to get acquainted with one another in more than a superficial way. It will also prepare the way for the decision about what to study together.

Studying a Book

Books are meant to be read from beginning to end. Can you imagine how confusing it would be to read a page out of *Tom Sawyer*, a line from *Hamlet*, then a paragraph from *War and Peace*? They wouldn't make any sense! Yet many people try to study the Bible that way. Book studies allow you to see biblical stories or ideas *in context* and to follow them from beginning to end.

If your group would like to study a biblical book, discuss which Old or New Testament books they are most interested in.

Keep in mind the needs of the group. If it consists of new Christians or people with only a vague grasp of Scripture, it would probably be unwise to study Ezekiel. Stick with something that is easier, shorter and more foundational.

The Gospel of Mark is a good place to learn more about the person and work of Christ. It is the shortest of the Gospels and is full of action.

Shorter New Testament epistles, such as Galatians, Ephesians, Philippians, Colossians, James and the letters of Peter, are also good choices. They are fairly easy to understand, and their message is basic and practical. For a leadership group, consider 1 and 2 Timothy or Titus.

Old Testament books such as Joshua, Ruth, 1 Samuel, Nehemiah, Amos and Jonah are popular. You might begin with something short, like Jonah or Ruth; then attempt something longer, such as Joshua or Nehemiah.

Studying a Character

Character studies can also be fascinating. Who can forget the stories of Noah and the flood, Abraham's sacrifice of Isaac, Joshua and the battle of Jericho, or Daniel in the lions' den? Character studies allow us to observe God at work in the lives of various men and women.

The Old Testament is a rich resource for character studies. Genesis, for example, looks at the lives of Abraham, Isaac, Jacob and Joseph. Moses is obviously the key figure in the book of Exodus. Judges looks at such people as Deborah, Gideon and Samson. First Samuel considers Hannah, Eli, Samuel, Saul and David. The books of Ruth, Nehemiah, Esther and Jonah are character studies in themselves.

The New Testament also contains many interesting characters. In the Gospels you might consider studying Mary the mother of Jesus, or

Joseph, her husband. Mary's relative Elizabeth and her husband, Zechariah, also have much to teach us. The sisters Mary and Martha of Bethany are popular for character studies too.

The book of Acts focuses primarily on the lives of Peter and Paul. But you also encounter such people as Stephen, Philip and the Ethiopian, Cornelius, Barnabas, Apollos, Priscilla and Aquila.

Studying a Topic

Some groups prefer to study a topic. Some basic ones to consider are evangelism, prayer and decision making. You might also study about Christian character, Christian disciplines, missions or social responsibility. Or you might want to study about a shared life experience like singleness or marriage.

Studying with Seekers

It can be a powerful experience for seekers to come together with Christians and study the Bible. Three LifeBuilders are designed especially with seekers in mind: *Meeting Jesus, Jesus the Reason* and *Encountering Jesus*. In each of these guides the study questions are appropriate for both seekers and Christians. And the applications are written with seekers in mind as well. Each focuses on the Gospels and is designed to present an opportunity for people to discover who Jesus is by reading the Bible for themselves.

Studying with a Guide

There are several important reasons for using a study guide as the basis for your discussion, whether you study a book, character or topic.

One important reason is time. It takes a considerable amount of time to write a good set of discussion questions. Three to four hours per week is probably the average. Most discussion leaders cannot easily afford that much time in preparation.

Another reason is quality. Those who write these guides are usually trained in Bible study and have some expertise in the subject they are writing about. On the other hand, it is the exceptional discussion leader who has both the skill and the knowledge to write an effective study guide.

Study guides also allow the group to prepare in advance. We strongly recommend that each member of the group has a guide. If they can study and make notes in the guide before the discussion, their preparation will greatly enhance your discussion. Even without preparation, the guide allows them to record insights during the study.

In a good study guide, the questions are clearly written, interesting and thought-provoking. Good questions generate discussion rather than simply call for one-word answers. They draw out the content and meaning of the passage. Each study will also have at least two or three questions that apply the passage to daily life.

There are ten to fourteen questions on the Scripture text, which is usually sufficient for a study lasting from forty-five minutes to an hour. (More time is needed for group discussion at the opening and prayer at the end.) If your time is limited, you may want to mark a couple of questions that can be skipped or summarized if necessary.

Be sure that the main impact of the study (often brought out by the final questions) is not missed!

LifeBuilders focus on only one or two passages per study rather than hopping from passage to passage, so that the group can focus on one particular part of Scripture at a time and thus begin to get a better picture of the whole.

Finally, look for the leader's notes at the back of each guide to give you added biblical background and tips on group dynamics.

Bring several different guides to the first meeting. You might spread them out on a table or pass them around. This usually makes it much easier for the group to decide what they want to study. Once they have chosen a guide, you can order a copy for each person.

Putting It Together

One small group chose to study 1 Timothy for the first few weeks. This provided a brief book, easy to get through—so only a short-term commitment was needed to get the group going. They then renewed the commitment and turned to the second part of the guide—2 Timothy and Titus. Then they wanted to spend some time in the Old Testament and studied Jonah. Character studies came next, focusing on the lives of David and the women of the New Testament. By then they had completed a year's worth of curriculum. With sixty-six books and so many characters and topics to choose from, they have only scratched the surface of what they may cover in the future!

3

Preparing to Lead

W hen I was growing up, my dad would sometimes teach Sunday school for a quarter. He would spend most of the day Saturday studying the Bible and commentaries and maps and such. On Sunday morning he was really ready to bring the lesson to life. I remember his careful preparation with respect and even awe.

Effective Bible study leadership demands preparation. But the difference between teaching a class and leading from a guide is that, with questions already provided for you, the time needed to do your best job is greatly reduced when you are using a guide. The preparation time needed to lead a LifeBuilder Bible Study (though this will vary from person to person) is thirty minutes to an hour. This time should be devoted to prayer and Bible study. If you keep to it faithfully, you will be confident and competent every time you lead a study.

Prayer

In John 15 Jesus gave us this warning: "Apart from me you can do nothing." Of course you *can* do something. You can carefully prepare and even lead an apparently effective study. But apart from the Lord, it will have no spiritual value. And most likely, lives will not be changed. Of course, God sometimes chooses to work through us despite our sin. But greater investment will bring greater growth. The Lord's presence with us will transform our efforts from mere activity into life-changing ministry.

Pray for yourself. Ask God to help you to understand the passage and apply it to your own life. Unless this happens, you will not be prepared to lead others. Ask God to help you understand both the passage and the study questions so you will be able to concentrate on helping the group members learn from Scripture. Ask him to fill you anew with his Spirit so you will be free from the self-consciousness that can so easily interfere with the work of God's Spirit in the group.

Pray for the members of the group. Think of them individually: their strengths, weaknesses, needs, interests and knowledge of Scripture. Pray that God will enable them to discover something of the richness and challenge of the passage. Let Paul's prayer be your model: "And this is my prayer: that your love may abound more and more in knowledge and depth of insight, so that you will be able to discern what is best and may be pure and blameless until the day of Christ, filled with the fruit of righteousness that comes through Jesus Christ—to the glory and praise of God" (Phil 1:9–10).

Bible Study

Having immersed yourself and the group in prayer, you are ready to begin studying. Martin Luther compared Bible study to gathering apples. "First I shake the whole tree, that the ripest may fall. Then I climb the tree and shake each limb, and then each branch and then each twig, and then I look under each leaf." Here's how you can follow his advice.

1. Read the introduction to the study guide. Then, if you are studying a Bible book, start by reading it from beginning to end. This overview will help you grasp the theme of the book. Ask yourself how each chapter contributes to that theme. Pay special attention to the context of the passage your group will be studying. If the book is too long to read in one sitting, scan its contents, paying special attention to paragraph and chapter headings.

2. Next, read and reread the passage for the study you will be leading. At this point your primary goal is to understand *what* the author was saying to the original readers and *why*.

3. While you study, have a dictionary and a Bible dictionary handy. Use them to look up any unfamiliar words, names or places.
4. Carefully work through each question in the study guide. Spend time in meditation and reflection as you formulate your responses. Philip Henry wrote, "A garment that is double dyed, dipped again and again, will retain the colour a great while; so a truth which is the subject of meditation."
5. Give particular attention to how this passage applies to your life. What encouragement, counsel, commands or promises does it offer? Remember that the group members will not share any more deeply from their own lives than you do. So be prepared to talk about what you are learning at a couple of key points.
6. Write your responses in the space provided in the study guide. Writing has an amazing effect on the mind. It forces us to think and to clearly express our understanding of the passage. It also helps us to remember what we have studied.
7. Familiarize yourself with the leader's notes written for the study you are leading. Such notes are usually designed to help you in several ways. First, they tell you the purpose the study guide author had in mind while writing the study. Take time to think through how the study questions work together to accomplish that purpose. Second, the notes provide you with additional background information or comments on some of the questions. This information can be useful if people have difficulty answering or understanding a question. Third, the leader's notes can alert you to potential problems you may encounter during the discussion. If you wish to remind yourself of anything mentioned in the leader's notes, make a note to yourself below that question in the study.

The Benefits of Preparation

The questions are designed to flow naturally out of the passage. You may feel that these studies lead themselves. But don't be fooled. It will feel easy and natural only when you have carefully prepared. When you feel confident and ready, you will be able to get your nose out of the guide and be attentive to the group members, encouraging everyone to interact and respond.

I would sometimes ask my dad how he felt about doing all that work for one Sunday school class, and he would always respond in the same way. He would tell me that it was a great opportunity for him to spend time studying the Bible. For him, teaching wasn't about receiving accolades for Bible knowledge or increasing Sunday school attendance with fascinating lesson plans; it was about the time with God. And the same benefit is available to us as we lead Bible studies.

4

Warming Up the Group

🕐 10 to 15 minutes of a group discussion
- Introduction
- Group Discussion
- Personal Reflection
- Opening Prayer

The moment has arrived. It's 6:30, and the meeting begins at 7:00. Don't panic. Instead, calmly take a last look around the room.

You want to create a comfortable setting for the discussion. If possible, choose a meeting space that is informal and attractive, such as a living room. Arrange the seats in a circle rather than rigid rows so people can have eye contact with each other. Make sure the room is well lit and the temperature is comfortable. Offer people refreshments, such as coffee, tea or soft drinks. (This can be done at the beginning or end of the meeting, or both.) You could pass around a bowl of popcorn for those who want to nibble. Have extra Bibles or printouts of the Bible text on hand. You might have an extra copy of the guide ready in case you have a visitor or a forgetful member.

Getting Started
Begin promptly at the announced time. If you wait for people to gather, they will acquire the habit of being late. Plan the early minutes carefully so they will be interesting and profitable to those who are prompt but not so crucial that latecomers will be hopelessly lost.

One way to deal with lateness is to announce that the group will gather at 7:00 so people can hang up their coats and get a cup of coffee. But also tell everyone ahead of time that the study itself will begin at 7:15. Then start the discussion promptly at the announced time.

Getting Acquainted
Make sure everyone knows each other. When group members are open with each other and relaxed in personal relationships, dynamic discussion and effective learning usually take place. When members are uneasy with one another, both the discussion and the learning process are hindered. After those present have been introduced to one another, address people by name to help others remember names.

Each study begins with a group discussion question to get people talking. However, you may want to do an icebreaker before that, depending on how well people know each other and how long you've been together. The *Small Group Starter Kit* (IVP, 1995) has lots of ideas in this area. Sometimes the group discussion section may serve as an icebreaker activity, so see what is suggested there and in any corresponding notes.

Early in your meetings together it will be important to take time each week to get to know each other. As time passes, people will connect and reconnect naturally as they come in and get ready for the study so you won't need a fun game to make this happen.

Introducing the Study
To illustrate how a LifeBuilder works, we are going to walk through an actual LifeBuilder study. It's study one of *God's Word*. The study title is "Longing for Christ."

The first paragraph or two in each study is an introduction designed to pique the group's interest. The first box on page 23 shows the introduction to "Longing for Christ." You can read the introduction aloud as it is written or ask a group member to read it. Or if you prefer, you can summarize the introduction and study theme briefly in your own words, drawing on (but not quoting verbatim) the purpose

---

INTRODUCTION

God's Word is alive. We experience the power of the living Word
when we read Scripture and are moved to follow its teachings
or when we study the Bible with others and discover new
truths about faith. And when we are able to encourage others
through the promises of Scripture, or—perhaps most
importantly—when the eyes of seekers are opened to see the
meaning of the biblical account of Christ's death and
resurrection, we experience the living Word.

---

statement for the study found in the leader's notes. Here is the purpose statement for "Longing for Christ":

PURPOSE

To discover how we meet Christ in the living Word of Scripture.

Sometimes the introduction is a personal anecdote from the life of the guide's writer. If you prefer, you can substitute your own story or something that you know will connect with your group. But it's also fine to use these anecdotes just as they are written.

What you are trying to do is to draw out a key theme from the study without giving away too much. The introduction should get the attention of the group members. And it may expose a personal need. If people feel that the passage will be speaking to a real concern or lack in their lives, they will be much more eager to study it.

The introduction opens up a question. It doesn't provide the answers.

Starting the Group Discussion

Next you will read the group discussion question. It is designed to help the group members to warm up to each other. No matter how well people may know each other or how comfortable they may be with each other, there is always a stiffness that needs to be overcome before people will begin to talk openly. Here's the question from our sample study.

GROUP DISCUSSION
When and how has Scripture come to life for you?

Whether it is a question or two or an activity, this part of the study is designed to get people thinking along the lines of the topic. Most people will have lots of different things going on in their minds (dinner, an important meeting coming up, how to get the car fixed) that have nothing to do with the study. A creative question will get their attention and draw them into the discussion.

This question can also reveal where our thoughts or feelings need to be transformed by Scripture. This is why it is especially important for the group *not* to read the passage before the opening group discussion question. The passage will tend to color the honest reactions people would otherwise give because they are of course *supposed* to think the way the Bible does. Giving honest responses to various issues before they find out what the Bible says may help them see where their thoughts or attitudes need to be changed.

Although you may want to drop icebreakers from your small group meetings as time passes, you will always want to take time for the group discussion question or activity. These few minutes will set the tone for the rest of the study.

Allowing for Personal Reflection

The personal reflection section is designed for individuals studying on their own. It is generally a question for thought or a topic for prayer. Here's the reflection from our *God's Word* sample study.

PERSONAL REFLECTION
Spend some time thanking God for what he
has taught you from Scripture thus far.

Some groups like to take a few minutes of quiet for each member to complete this section on their own. Simply allow three minutes or so of silence, then ask people if they want to talk about what they experienced during this time—no pressure—and move on to the next part of the study.

Depending on the personal preferences and comfort level of your group with silence, you might like to try this. It can help people to stop and quiet themselves in the midst of the busyness of life in order to be more prepared to focus on the Scripture. It can help people to learn disciplines of silence and reflection in their own lives. This may be something you want to try only after your group has been together for a while.

Opening Prayer
This will be a good point at which to offer a brief prayer for your group. It will prepare the group to hear and receive the Scripture. Though it's always nice to draw in group members, it may be appropriate for you to pray since you will have your hopes and goals for the study in mind. Ask the Spirit to be present and to reveal the truths of the Word to you. Keep it short here and plan to allow a longer period for group prayer at the end of the study. Prayer will also help the group transition from the introductory time to the text at hand.

5

Getting Inside
the Passage

⏱ 10 to 15 minutes of a group discussion
- Introducing the Bible Text
- Reading the Passage
- Connecting to the Scripture
- Overview Questions

A New York Times advertisement of Mortimer Adler's *How to Read a Book* had a picture of a puzzled adolescent reading a letter. The ad copy read as follows:

How to Read a Love Letter
This young man has just received his first love letter. He may have read it three or four times, but he is just beginning. To read it as accurately as he would like would require several dictionaries and a good deal of close work with a few experts of etymology and philology. However, he will do all right without them.

He will ponder over the exact shade of meaning of every word, every comma. She has headed the letter, "Dear John." What, he asks himself, is the exact significance of those words? Did she refrain from saying "Dearest" because she was bashful? Would "My Dear" have sounded too formal?

Jeepers, maybe she would have said "Dear So-and-So" to anybody! A worried frown will now appear on his face. But it disappears as soon as he really gets to thinking about the first sentence. She certainly wouldn't have written *that* to anybody!

And so he works his way through the letter, one moment perched blissfully on a cloud, the next moment huddled miserably behind an eight ball. It has started a hundred questions in his mind. He could quote it by heart. In fact, he will—to himself—for weeks to come.

The advertisement concludes: "If people read books with anything like the same concentration, we'd be a race of mental giants."*

Making the Connection

Your task is to foster in your group the kind of passion for Scripture that reading a love letter instills in the beloved. You will take the need that the introduction opened up and dive into Scripture to find comfort, hope and answers.

In our sample study the group is being stimulated by a reminder of the life and power that we find in God's Word. We receive a promise that we will meet Jesus there. Usually it's just a sentence that makes the transition from the topic to the text.

TRANSITION TO TEXT

John 1 describes how the Word (God's message to the people of planet earth) was revealed to us in Christ. *Read John 1:1–5, 14–18.*

Reading the Text

The authors of LifeBuilder Bible Studies use the New International Version of the Bible. This means that when they quote from Scripture they quote from the NIV. So the simplest thing will be to use the NIV. To get away from confusion and tangents caused by differing versions

---

* As quoted by Robert A. Traina, *Methodical Bible Study* (Wilmore, Ky.: Asbury Theological Seminary, 1952), pp. 97–98.

and study Bible notes as well as to make seekers and young Christians more comfortable, I often print out copies of the section to be studied for my group. The complete NIV text is available on the Bible Gateway at <www.biblegateway.com>. LifeBuilders are also easily compatible with the NRSV and TNIV. Other versions of Scripture will work fine with these studies as well. For many Christians the KJV or NASB remains the version they most trust, so feel free to use these guides with the text that is appropriate to your context.

If there is someone in the group who you think would be comfortable reading this text as a unit, ask him or her to do that. Some groups go around a circle with everyone reading a verse. This can be good for longer sections—where you are covering a chapter or two. But there are inevitable bumps as versions vary and people lose their places. Further, some people are more comfortable reading aloud than others are, especially when biblical language may be unfamiliar. For shorter readings it will be smoothest to simply ask one person to read through the text.

When you study a historical narrative, such as those found in the Gospels and Acts, it is sometimes fun to read it dramatically. Assign parts for the various characters in the story. This can bring a passage to life and give you a sense of being there.

In some studies where the text is long or complicated, the reading may be broken into sections. In such a case you will be instructed to read at a couple points. In most cases it's best to read it all through as a unit to get the whole teaching or story as a complete thought.

In case you haven't opened your Bible yet, here is the text so that you can follow the logic of the rest of the sample study from *God's Word*.

> ¹In the beginning was the Word, and the Word was with God, and the Word was God. ²He was with God in the beginning.
>
> ³Through him all things were made; without him nothing was made that has been made. ⁴In him was life, and that life was the light of men. ⁵The light shines in the darkness, but the darkness has not understood it.

¹⁴The Word became flesh and made his dwelling among us. We have seen his glory, the glory of the One and Only, who came from the Father, full of grace and truth.

¹⁵John testifies concerning him. He cries out, saying, "This was he of whom I said, 'He who comes after me has surpassed me because he was before me.'" ¹⁶From the fullness of his grace we have all received one blessing after another. ¹⁷For the law was given through Moses; grace and truth came through Jesus Christ. ¹⁸No one has ever seen God, but God the One and Only, who is at the Father's side, has made him known. (Jn 1:1–5, 14–18)

The Overview Question

The first question after the text is read is designed to give an overview of what is happening in the passage. It is a fact-based question that should direct people to give answers directly from the Scripture. Here's what the leader's note for question 1 of this study says.

This overview question is designed to give a brief overview of the themes of the passage. We'll go into more detail on each verse later, so don't dwell on this too long.

> THE OVERVIEW QUESTION
> 1. What do we learn about the Word in these verses?

The question will generally draw on all of the passage to help people get clear about what's going on. Stay on the surface with this observation question. This is not the time for in-depth interpretation. More on observation and interpretation in the next chapter!

Getting Inside the Passage

The next two questions are designed to help the group connect to what is going on in the verses. In this case question 2 is an observation question that points to how we see God. Question 3 asks for a personal response to what is happening in the text.

In a narrative study there will often be a question about what it would be like to be present as one of the characters. In such cases the

GETTING INSIDE THE PASSAGE

2. What do God's actions in these verses reveal about his character?

3. How do you respond to this picture of Christ as the Word?

overview question may also be a question that gets the reader inside the text so that both purposes are served by one question.

Getting inside the passage, perhaps the most critical step for contemporary readers, is what helps us relate to what is going on. Many will not engage until they feel connected. When we get inside the passage, we have an opportunity to become God's beloved children reading a love letter from our Father. Excitement builds and we are motivated to discover what is in that letter and what it really means.

6

Uncovering the Meaning

⏲ 30 minutes of a group discussion
  • Observation Questions
  • Interpretation Questions
  • Leader's Notes

In order to read the Bible with understanding, we need to answer three primary questions: (1) What does it *say*? (2) What does it *mean*? (3) What does it mean to *me*?

Answering the first question requires *observation*.

Answering the second question requires *interpretation*.

Answering the third question requires *application*.

In this chapter we'll cover observation and interpretation. In the next chapter we'll cover application.

Observation

Sherlock Holmes was known for his brilliant powers of observation. One day a stranger came into Holmes's study. The detective looked over the gentleman carefully then remarked to Watson: "Beyond the obvious facts that he has at some time done manual labour, that he takes snuff, that he is a Freemason, that he has been in China, and that he has done considerable amount of writing lately, I can deduce nothing else."

Watson was so astounded by his abilities that he commented: "I could not help laughing at the ease with which he explained his process of deduction. 'When I hear you give your reasons,' I remarked, 'the thing always appears to me to be so ridiculously simple that I could easily do it myself, though at each successive instance of your reasoning I am baffled, until you explain your process. And yet I believe that my eyes are as good as yours.'

"'Quite so,' he answered . . . throwing himself down into an armchair. 'You see, but you do not *observe*.'"*

The first step in personal Bible study is to make several *observations* about the passage or book you are studying. Questions 1 and 2 of our sample study were observation questions. Observation is about seeing the obvious and the not so obvious. We bombard the book or passage with questions.

1. *Who:* Who is the author of the book? Who is being addressed? Who are the major and minor characters?
2. *Where:* Where do the events occur? Are there any references to towns, cities, provinces? If so, look these up in a Bible atlas or on a map. (Many Bibles include maps.) If you are reading a letter, where do the recipients live?
3. *When:* Are there any references to the time, day, month or year, or to when events took place in relation to other events?
4. *What:* What actions or events are taking place? What words or ideas are repeated or are central to the passage? What is the mood (joyous, somber)?
5. *Why:* Does the passage offer any reasons, explanations, statements of purpose?
6. *How:* How is the passage written? Is it a letter, speech, poem, parable? Does the author use any figures of speech (similes, metaphors)? How is it organized (around ideas, people, geography)?

By probing a book or passage with questions, you will uncover many important facts. The importance of careful observation cannot be

* *The Illustrated Sherlock Holmes Treasury* (New York: Avenel, 1976), pp. 17, 2.

overstressed since your observations will form the basis for your interpretations.

Good observation questions should cause the group to search the passage and its context. They should not be so simple or superficial that they can be answered with one- or two-word answers. Sometimes the group will quit responding too quickly. LifeBuilder questions should generate more than one response. Encourage the group to dig deeper, inviting others to contribute.

Some may feel that observation questions are dull. Help the group to understand what they accomplish. Observation is particularly valuable for seekers and newer Christians who need to get the basics down. You may find that these group members respond most readily to observation questions because they can see that they have the "right answer." More mature Christians may have learned to make the observations intuitively and be ready to jump to interpretation. Observation levels the playing field. Further, long-time Christians can miss important elements because they think they already know the passage well.

The language of the Bible is rich and multilayered. Each of us can be enriched by dwelling on the words before jumping to the meaning.

Interpretation

The second step in Bible study is interpretation. This type of question follows after we have had an opportunity to make some observations and get inside the text. Questions 4 and 5 of the sample study from *God's Word* are interpretation questions.

INTERPRETATION

4. Why do you think the name "the Word" is used here?

5. Why is the role of the Word in creation emphasized so strongly (vv. 1–4)?

Interpretation seeks to understand the facts that have been uncovered.

Were there any words you didn't understand? Define them.

Did the author use figurative language? This needs to be unraveled.

Were major ideas presented? Try to grasp their meaning and significance.

Did you encounter any difficulties? Seek to resolve them.

Meaning, significance, explanation—these are the goals of the interpreter. How do you reach these goals? And once you have reached them, how do you know you are not mistaken?

For example, have you ever been discussing a passage of Scripture with someone when suddenly he or she says, "That's just your interpretation," as if to say, "You have your interpretation and I have mine, and mine is just as good as yours!"

People often disagree on how the Bible should be interpreted. And there are some issues that we won't feel resolved about until we meet God in heaven. But good interpretation follows careful observation because the key is discovering the author's intended meaning.

How Do You Handle the Tough Interpretation Questions?

First, try to anticipate the questions when you prepare. After you've studied the passage on your own, read the leader's notes and see what further background or insight is offered there. Often the notes will give extra help where disagreement on interpretation can be expected. In the sample study the following notes are provided for questions 4 and 5 to help in the interpretation process.

If you have a question that you still don't feel has been answered, then check a study Bible or commentary or ask a friend for help.

If you get into a controversy in the study, remember that controversy can be very stimulating! Allow people to share their thoughts freely. Avoid imposing your particular view on the group. When you sense that you aren't getting any further with the issue or that people are getting frustrated, encourage the group to agree to disagree and move on. You might keep the issue in mind as a topic that you can explore more deeply later, or you might encourage people to study more on their own.

LEADER'S NOTES

Question 4. If people find this difficult, you may want to read them the following quote from *The NIV Study Bible* and discuss it.

> Greeks used this term not only of the spoken word but also of the unspoken word, the word still in the mind—the reason. When they applied it to the universe, they meant the rational principle that governs all things. Jews, on the other hand, used it as a way of referring to God. Thus John used a term that was meaningful to both Jews and Gentiles. (Kenneth Barker, ed. [Grand Rapids, Mich.: Zondervan, 1995], p. 1590)

Question 5. Note in Genesis 1 how, as God speaks, each aspect of the world comes into being. We may think of a word as passive ink on a page, but this is a Word with power—the power to bring us into existence.

Once you learn how to observe and interpret Scripture, you will discover that you are using these good reading principles each time you read the Bible and that God's Word is alive in your life.

7

Making It Real

⏱ 10 to 30 minutes of a group discussion
- Application Questions
- Summary Questions
- Praying Together

The ultimate purpose of Bible study is not simply to educate us but to *transform* us. In Romans 12:2 Paul gives us this exhortation: "Do not conform any longer to the pattern of this world, but be transformed by the renewing of your mind." As we renew our minds through the study of Scripture, the Holy Spirit gradually transforms us into the image of Jesus Christ.

Principles of Application
To properly apply the Scriptures, we must remember the nature of Scripture. Almost every book of the Bible was written to address specific problems, needs and questions of the people living *at that time*. For example, the believers in Corinth had problems of division, immorality, marriage, food sacrificed to idols, spiritual gifts and lawsuits among believers. Paul wrote 1 Corinthians to answer their specific questions. We face many of these same problems and questions today. It is still possible to take another believer to court, and we still have questions about marriage. In fact there are hundreds of ways in which our problems and needs correspond to those faced by the people in the Bible. This is natural since we share a common humanity. And it leads us to the first principle of application.

Rule #1: *Whenever our situation corresponds to that faced by the original readers, God's Word to us is exactly the same as it was to them.*

But there are also situations from their day which do not have an exact counterpart today. This, too, is to be expected because of the differences between modern and biblical culture. For example, almost no one in our society sacrifices food to idols. In such cases we should follow the second principle of application.

Rule #2: *Whenever our situation does not correspond to that faced by the original readers, we should look for the* principle *underlying God's Word to them. We can then apply that principle to comparable situations today.*

What was the principle underlying Paul's words about food sacrificed to idols? He was concerned that the Corinthians not do anything that would lead someone with a weak conscience to sin: "Therefore, if what I eat causes my brother to fall into sin, I will never eat meat again, so that I will not cause him to fall" (1 Cor 8:13). This principle might be applicable to many situations today, such as whether a Christian should drink alcoholic beverages around someone who is a former alcoholic—or drink at all.

Flowing into Application

Bible study without application is an intellectual exercise that fails to call us to accountability and growth. LifeBuilders exercise both the mind and the spirit. Accurate application builds on careful observation

---

FLOWING INTO APPLICATION

6. In what ways do people today fail to see the light shining through the darkness?

7. What do you find significant about the fact that the Word became flesh (v. 4)?

8. What are some ways that we see God's glory?

9. How can we, like John (v. 15), declare Christ's glory to others?

10. How is the law a precursor to Jesus, the Word?

and interpretation, so we generally put the first application question in at about question 5 or 6. In our sample study, question 6 is the first application question in a series.

Question 7 calls for interpretation, and it is then followed by two more application questions. Question 10 is another interpretation question. So it's not a structured kind of study in which we do all the observation, all the interpretation and then all the application. There's an interplay of all these dynamics flowing through the study as the questions surface naturally from the text. Sometimes there are combination questions that call you to do a bit of observation and then make an application and so on.

How Do I Apply the Bible to My Life?

Once you understand these principles of application, you can think of unlimited ways in which God's Word applies today. You can ask such questions as:

- Is there a command for me to obey?
- Is there a promise to claim?
- Is there an example to follow?
- Is there a sin to avoid or confess?
- Is there a reason for thanksgiving or praise?
- What does this passage teach me about God, Jesus, myself, others?

Wrapping Up

A summary question helps you look back though the whole text to draw together the main points of a passage or book. The summary

---

WRAPPING UP

11. We read in four different verses that the Word was with God. Why is this point emphasized?

12. How can regarding Scripture as God's living Word impact the way you handle it?

---

question could be an observation or interpretation question, but not every study has one of these—especially when there's a lot of text to cover. Sometimes it's an application question that draws out the main themes of the text. In the sample study from *God's Word* question 11 is an interpretation question that calls for a review of the text. After gathering responses to this question, it would also be appropriate for you as the leader to take a minute to summarize the highlights of your discussion. Then ask the final application question.

This question will make the study personal and will generally call for a personal commitment in response to the study. It often ties into the prayer suggestion, which you can use in closing your time together.

8

Following Up

⏱ 5 to 20 minutes of a group discussion
- Closing in Prayer
- Now or Later

My first experience of Christians praying out loud together in an informal way (rather than formal church prayers given from a podium) was in my first small group. At first I found it intimidating and awkward, but gradually I became more comfortable. Over time I found that my own prayer life and vocabulary were growing as I learned how to pray by listening to others pray. I learned that God understands ordinary language. And I found that verbalizing my own prayers helped me to be aware of how I was praying and what I was asking for! So I strongly encourage you to take time to pray with your group—whether it's five minutes or fifteen minutes.

Closing in Prayer
Prayer suggestions are found in italics at the end of each study. They are intentionally simple and open-ended to provide a theme or direction for prayer that will tie into the study and to remind you to pray. You should pray as you feel led according to what has taken place in your study. In this case the guide says:

Ask God to be with you as you continue to study his Word and to impress his truth on your heart.

If most or all of your group members are Christians and you've been together for a few weeks, then you may want to try praying aloud together, using "conversational prayer." Conversational prayer includes the following components:

- listing some topics for prayer
- praying for one topic at a time with a variety of people praying for aspects of that topic
- often praying short prayers, possibly just adding a phrase to another's prayer. Individual prayers in this format don't end "in Jesus' name." This phrase is used at the end of the whole "conversation," as the group is creating one long prayer together.
- speaking naturally to Jesus as if he were in the center of the circle.*

To ease the group into praying aloud together, you might try offering prayers that people can chime in and complete, like "We thank you for . . ." or "We pray for our family and friends . . ." and so on. Or you can ask for prayer requests and ask each person to pray for the request made by the person to their right. It is a powerful experience to hear someone pray for our needs. Doing this will knit your group together and grow the members spiritually.

Now or Later

At the end of each study you will find a section called "Now or Later." This section expands on the themes of the study through further Scripture reading, discussion, meditation, journaling or taking action to apply the passage. Many of the ideas are most effective when individuals or prayer partners carry them out between sessions. However, you can work on them in group meetings as well, if time allows. Here's the "Now or Later" idea from the *God's Word* sample study.

To help people apply what they are learning, you may want to encourage group members to work on these ideas between studies,

---

* Ann Beyerlein, in *Small Group Leaders' Handbook*, ed. Jimmy Long (Downers Grove, Ill.: InterVarsity Press, 1995), p. 79.

NOW OR LATER

Read these verses in a couple different Bible versions, especially a paraphrase like *The Message* or the New Living Translation. Note the words or images that stand out. How is your understanding of this passage deepened or expanded?

then ask at the beginning or end of the next study what they are learning. Even if you don't use the "Now or Later" section, you may want to ask follow-up questions about key points of application from the previous studies. You won't need to do this every week, but you may sense key points in group life where people are experiencing spiritual transformation and making potentially life-changing decisions. Simply moving on to the next topic without any follow-up would be neglecting what is happening spiritually at those points.

9

Leading the
Discussion

Good Bible study leaders are facilitators. They strike the match that ignites the group—primarily by affirming the members of the group and encouraging them to participate. Your attitude as the leader is one of the most significant factors in determining the spirit and tone of the discussion. Your respect for the authority of the Bible will be contagious even though you may never express it in words. Your love and openness toward people in the group will quickly infect those around you. Your relaxed attitude and genuine enjoyment of the discussion will spread to every group member from the start of the discussion.

Guidelines for Discussion
At the beginning of your first time together, explain that these studies are meant to be discussions, not lectures. Then read or summarize the following guidelines for Bible discussions from the LifeBuilder leader's notes.

- Try to stick to the topic being studied.
- Your responses should be based on the verses that are the focus of the discussion and not on outside authorities such as commentaries or speakers.

- These studies focus on a particular passage of Scripture. Only rarely should you refer to other portions of the Bible. This allows for everyone to participate in in-depth study on equal ground.
- Anything said in the group is considered confidential and will not be discussed outside the group unless specific permission is given to do so.
- Listen attentively to each other and provide time for each person present to talk.
- Pray for each other.

Agree on how the guides are to be used by the group members. Do you want them to prepare before the study? If you have group members who want to prepare ahead of the study, that's great! It will allow you to go deeper in the study session. At the same time, one of the nice things about these studies is that group members can get a lot out of them without any preparation. So I never push preparation, and I always encourage people to come whether prepared or not. As a matter of fact, I've never been in a group where people did consistently prepare—but I've been in groups with consistent (guilt-free) attendance, and we've had lots of great discussions.

Reading the Questions

As you begin to ask the group the questions in the guide, it will be helpful to keep several things in mind. First, the questions can often be used just as they are written. If you wish, you may simply read them aloud to the group (but omit the question number). Or you may prefer to express them in your own words. However, unnecessary rewording of the questions is not recommended, as the questions have been field-tested by various groups and revised prior to publication. Although I have led studies for many years, I find that when I attempt to reword or create a new question on the spot, I often create a yes/no question that doesn't generate a strong response.

There may be times when it is appropriate to deviate from the study guide. For example, a question may already have been answered. If so, move on to the next question. Or someone may raise an important question not covered in the guide. Take time to discuss it! The important thing is to use discretion. There may be many routes you can travel to reach the goal of the study. But the easiest route is usually the one the author has suggested.

If your group does prepare ahead, beware of people getting their noses stuck in their guides and saying, "I wrote _____ for question 8." You want to create a discussion with dialogue and inter-action. People will discover more as they listen to one another. If necessary, you might ask the group to put away their guides.

Talking Points

A professor once told me, "The hardest thing about teaching is not answering your own questions." Indeed, it is hard when you read the carefully crafted question and the group members just stare at you. Here are a few tips for helping people to talk.

1. Avoid answering your own questions! If necessary, repeat or rephrase the question until it is clearly understood. An eager group quickly becomes passive and silent if they think the leader will do most of the talking. The exceptions can be the group discussion question at the beginning and the application questions. It may help if you open up first.

2. Don't be afraid of silence. People need time to think about the question before formulating their answers. But try to discern the dif-ference between fruitful silence (when people are thinking) and blanks (when your question seems unclear or irrelevant).

3. Don't be content with just one answer. All of these questions should have more than one answer. Additional contributions will usually add depth and richness to the discussion. Ask, "What do the rest of you think?" or "Anything else?" until several people have had a chance to speak.

4. Be affirming! People will contribute much more eagerly if they feel their answers are genuinely appreciated. One way to be affirming is

to listen attentively whenever anyone speaks. Another is to verbally acknowledge their contribution. Respond to their answers by saying, "That's a good observation" or "Excellent point." Be especially affirming to shy or hesitant members of the group.

5. Be willing to admit your own ignorance or faults. It is easy for leaders to feel that they must have answers to all questions raised. If a wrong answer is given, or if a leader makes a mistake and fails to admit it, community spirit will be hindered. Admitting our faults and weaknesses will often release the entire group to a new level of openness to God's grace and to one another.

6. Periodically summarize what the *group* has said about the passage. This helps to draw together the various ideas mentioned and gives continuity to the study. But don't preach.

7. Foster group ownership by asking people (who you think would be comfortable) to read the study introduction, read the passage or pray. The healthiest group Bible studies are those in which all participants consider the study theirs. Invitations of "Come to our study" rather than "Come to Jane's study" are a sign that members have a sense of ownership. Generally, members who consider the study theirs will contribute more responsibly, prepare more thoroughly, invite others more freely and pray for the study more faithfully.

8. An ideal Bible study group includes eight to ten people. If the group experiences growth, as well-led groups often do, members should consider dividing into two groups when there are more than twelve people. In the smaller groups, each member will have an opportunity for more frequent participation. To make a successful division, prepare carefully and openly well in advance. Groom a new leader who will have an opportunity to lead the group before the split so that those who will be joining that leader's group will be acquainted with him or her. If space allows, some groups avoid the trauma of separation by meeting together in a common place and then splitting into different groups for the study. Others occasionally reassemble to share what God has been teaching them, thus keeping ties with the original members.

Handling Problems

Problems may arise in any discussion. If they are handled properly, however, they need not hurt the quality of the study.

What do you do, for example, if someone tries to monopolize the discussion? You might respond by saying, "Why don't we find out what some of the others think?" You might also direct your next question to those who have not been able to participate: "Why don't we hear from those who haven't spoken yet?" If the problem persists, try talking with the person privately after the study. Help the person to understand the importance of balanced participation. Ask for his or her help in drawing out the more quiet members of the group.

How should you respond to answers that are blatantly wrong? Never simply reject a comment. If it is obviously wrong, you could point the person back to Scripture, saying, "Which verse led you to that conclusion?" Or let the group handle the problem. Ask, "What do the rest of you think about this?" Their response will usually be sufficient for clearing up the misunderstanding.

What if the group goes off on a tangent? Encourage people to return to the passage under consideration. It should be the source for answering questions. Unnecessary cross-referencing should also be avoided.

Don't ignore problems. Deal with them in the group or in private, but do deal with them. Confronting one another in love requires God's grace and wisdom. But if someone is regularly frightening off new Christians or continually harangues the group with his or her own pet ideas, action may be needed. Always communicate acceptance of the person but realize that if nothing is done, the group could wither and die.

Following the suggestions given in this chapter should help you lead an enjoyable and profitable discussion. But leading a study should also be a *learning* experience for you. Even the most effective leader can always find room for improvement! It is helpful, therefore, to evaluate the study and your leadership once the discussion has concluded.

10

Evaluating
the Discussion

A good small group Bible study is like a popcorn popper. At first there are only a few pops as one or two people warm up to the group. Pretty soon, however, there is an explosion of sound as everyone begins to comment.

A poor Bible study is like a popcorn popper with a damaged heater. The group never warms up. Awkward silences are broken only occasionally by a cough or a lifeless, one-word answer.

What makes the difference between a good Bible study and a poor one? This chapter will help you and your group to discover the qualities of a great discussion.

The Leader

An evaluation is not a score of your performance. ("And here are the judges' votes: 6.0, 5.5, 5.5, 5.8 and 5.9.") It is primarily a *learning* experience that helps you identify the strengths and weaknesses of your leadership so you can do even better next time.

After the discussion, answer the following questions as objectively as possible. As you do so, ask God to show you any improvements or changes you need to make. If you want to, you could ask one or more of your group members to help you answer. Or if you have a small group coach, ask him or her to visit the group, and then work through this list together.

- Were you well prepared, having devoted a sufficient amount of time to prayer and study?
- Did you have a good grasp of the passage?
- Were you familiar with the questions and the leader's notes?
- Were you comfortable in your role as leader? Why or why not?
- Did you provide an adequate introduction to the study?
- Did you give people time to think about each question?
- Did you rephrase any unclear questions?
- Did you encourage more than one response to each question?
- Did you actively listen to each person's comments?
- Did you respond to these comments in an affirming manner?
- Did you ever answer your own question?
- Did you keep the discussion moving at an appropriate pace?
- Did you handle problems effectively?
- Did you begin and end the discussion on time?
- What can you do to improve the quality of your leadership next time?

These questions can also help you mentor a new discussion leader. Talk these items through before (as preparation) and after he or she leads a study.

The Group

The members of the group also have an important responsibility. An eager group can make the difference between a vibrant, dynamic discussion and one that administers general anesthesia. After your group has completed a series of studies, or if the discussions tend to drag, spend a few minutes evaluating their participation together.

- Are we at ease with each other?
- (if appropriate) Do we come to the meeting prepared?
- Do certain members tend to dominate the discussion?
- Do others tend to remain silent?
- Are most of the responses directed to the leader or do we interact with each other freely?

- Do we actively listen to each other's comments?
- Do we respond to these comments in an affirming manner?
- If any problems or controversies arise, do we handle them effectively, or do we leave this to the leader?
- Is our meeting room comfortable and pleasant?
- How could we improve the quality of our participation?

Working through these questions together will help the group to bond more deeply and to become more aware of how they can take initiative in the life of the group.

The Agony and the Joy

You will probably have your ups and downs with small group leading. I know I do. Some weeks I feel frustrated with the planning and with the personalities. I wonder: *Why is she always late? Why does he forget it's meeting night unless I call? Why doesn't she ever pray? Does anyone in my group really want to grow in Christ?*

And yet despite all the questions and frustrations, once we are gathered and small group begins, I'm always glad we are together. I learn something. I am drawn to Christ. I am reminded of my sin. I am grateful for the experience of community.

So keep leading. Small group life is just a taste of the rich community we will have in heaven. Its goodness enriches our lives here on earth and helps us find our way to God.

Guidelines to Interpreting Scripture

How can we discover the author's meaning? Here are five steps that will help you in making accurate interpretations of books of the Bible.

1. Discover the historical context of the book you are studying.
2. Identify the type of literature it is.
3. Get an overview of the book.
4. Study the book passage by passage.
5. Compare your interpretation with a good commentary.

1. Discover the Historical Context

The events described in the Bible took place thousands of years ago. This creates one obvious problem for understanding these events: we weren't there! Therefore, we often lack important information regarding the background or context in which these events took place.

For example, almost every New Testament letter was written to address a particular problem or set of problems: the Galatians were seeking to be justified by law; the Corinthians needed answers to questions about marriage, spiritual gifts, meat offered to idols and so on; Timothy needed to know how to restore order to a church.

Unless we understand these problems or questions, the letters are like listening to one end of a telephone conversation. We hear what the author is saying, but we don't know why he is saying it. The same is true when we read other books of the Bible. We know only half of the story!

One way to learn about the background or context of a psalm, prophetic book or New Testament letter is to look for clues within the book or passage itself. For example, in 1 John we read, "I am writing these things to you about those who are trying to lead you astray" (1 Jn 2:26). As we look elsewhere in the letter we discover that these false teachers had originally been part of the church: "They went out from us, but they did not really belong to us" (2:19). John calls them "antichrists" (2:18). There are many other statements, some explicit and some implicit, which give us additional details about the situation that John's readers faced.

Once you have looked within the book or passage itself, it is helpful to consult a Bible dictionary or handbook. For example, under the listing "John, Epistles of" you will find further information about the background and circumstances of 1 John.

It is also a good idea to read related passages in the Bible. For example, Psalm 51 was written by David after his adultery with Bathsheba. We can read the background about David and Bathsheba in 2 Samuel 11 – 12. (In Psalm 51 the heading over the psalm tells us why it was written. When such information isn't given, a Bible dictionary will often mention related passages.) Similarly, if you are studying Philippians, you will want to consult the book of Acts, which provides information about the founding of the church at Philippi (Acts 16).

The more you know about the historical context of a biblical passage, the better equipped you will be to understand the message of the author. Such information can be like finding missing pieces of a puzzle. As they are put into place, the whole picture becomes clearer.

2. Identify the Type of Literature You Are Studying

The biblical authors communicated in a variety of ways—through stories, letters, poems, proverbs, parables and symbols. The way they say things adds richness and beauty to *what* they say.

The literature of the Bible has been classified into various types. These include:

Discourse. The New Testament epistles are the clearest examples of discourse, an extended, logical discussion of a subject. Some of the prophetic sermons and the longer sermons of Jesus also fall into this category.

Prose narrative. This is the style used in books such as Genesis, Joshua and the Gospels. The author describes and recreates theologically significant scenes and events from biblical history.

Poetry. The Psalms, of course, fit in this category. Poetry uses figurative language. It also uses different types of parallelism and is emotional in nature.

Proverbs. Proverbs, such as those in the book of Proverbs, are wise sayings. They are practical *principles* for living. They should not be confused with commands or promises.

Parables. Jesus used parables more than anyone else in Scripture did. A parable explains a spiritual truth by means of a story or analogy. It is an extended simile or metaphor.

Prophetic literature. The prophetic books include the four major prophets (Isaiah, Jeremiah, Ezekiel and Daniel) and the twelve minor prophets (Hosea, Joel, and Amos through Malachi). The prophets were spokesmen for God who announced the curses and blessings associated with God's covenant with Israel.

Apocalyptic literature. The books of Daniel and Revelation are a special type of prophecy known as apocalyptic literature. The word *apocalypse* means to "uncover" or "reveal" something that is hidden. One distinct feature of these books is their heavy use of symbols.

Once you have identified the type of literature you are studying, consult a Bible dictionary. For example, if you are studying the Psalms, it would be wise to read an article on Hebrew poetry in order to learn how it is put together. Likewise, if you are studying Revelation, read an article on apocalyptic literature. It will explain why this kind of literature seems so strange to us and will offer suggestions for interpreting it correctly.

3. Get an Overview of the Book

On a large windswept plain in Peru, archeologists discovered a vast series of strange lines covering an area thirty-seven miles long. The archeologists first thought these lines were ancient roads. It wasn't until they happened to fly over the area in an airplane that they discovered their true significance. The lines joined to form a design, an immense mural that could only be seen from high above.

In Bible study it is helpful to get an overview of the book you are studying. The parts of the book only take on their true significance in light of the whole. But remember that the way a book is put together will be closely related to its literary type. An epistle such as Romans is organized around ideas. Historical narratives are put together in a variety of ways. Genesis (after chapter 11) is organized around people: Abraham, Isaac, Jacob and Joseph. Exodus is organized around geographical locations and events: in Egypt, en route to Sinai and then at Sinai. The Gospel of John focuses primarily on several "signs" which Jesus did. Psalm 119 is structured around the letters of the Hebrew alphabet!

1. *Begin by reading quickly through the book.* As you read, try to discover its overall theme. For example, the theme of Romans is righteousness by faith. When it isn't possible to read the entire book in one sitting, skim through its contents, paying particular attention to any chapter or paragraph headings contained in your Bible.

2. *Next, look for major sections or divisions within the book.* For example, the major divisions of Romans are chapters 1–5, 6–8, 9–11 and 12–16. Each of these sections focuses primarily on one subject. Once you have discovered that subject, try to summarize it by giving a brief descriptive title to the section. The various sections of

Romans could be entitled something like this: Being Declared Just (1–5), Being Made Holy (6–8), God's Dealings with Israel (9–11) and Living as Christians (12–16).

3. *Now look for subsections*—those major ideas that join together to form sections. The first section of Romans divides in two. Romans 1:18 – 3:20 describes the universal need for righteousness. Romans 3:21 – 5:21 describes how God declares us righteous through Jesus Christ.

4. *At each step of the way look for connections or relationships between the sections, subsections and paragraphs.* For example, Romans 1:18 – 3:20 is related to 3:21 – 5:21 because the former describes the *need* of humanity and the latter shows God's *solution* to that need. Other connections you might look for include things that are alike, things that are opposite, cause and effect, movement from general to specific and so on. Continually ask yourself how these paragraphs, subsections and sections contribute to the overall theme of the book.

In other words, an overview is like looking through a zoom lens. You begin with a panoramic view through the lens (reading the entire book), then zoom in for a closer look (identifying major sections), then still closer (looking for subsections). Now you are ready to focus closely on the paragraphs, sentences and words.

The more times you read a book, the more familiar you will become with its structure and contents. Your original overview will help you understand the *whole* of the book. This understanding will tend to affect the way you interpret its parts. But as you gain familiarity with the *parts*, your understanding of the whole may need to be modified, and so on. Each time you go through this cycle, you will come closer and closer to grasping the meaning of the author.

4. Study the Book Passage by Passage

Once you have an overview of the structure and contents of a book, begin studying it passage by passage. In our modern Bibles a passage can be a paragraph, a group of paragraphs or a chapter. Realize, however, that the Bible did not originally contain chapters, paragraphs or verses (or even punctuation!). These are helpful additions to our Bibles, but we need not be bound by them.

a. Read and reread the passage in order to familiarize yourself with its contents. As you read, look for the main *subject* of the passage.

b. Once you have identified the main subject, find out what the author is *saying* about it. If you are studying a paragraph, ask how the verses expand and explain the main subject of the paragraph. If you are studying a group of paragraphs, ask how each paragraph contributes to the main theme of that group. Do the same thing if you are studying a chapter.

c. Pay attention to the *context* of the passage you are studying. Read the verses or paragraphs immediately before and after the passage. Ask, "Why is this verse or paragraph here? How does the author use it to make his point clearer?" Keep in mind how the passage is related to the overall argument or theme of the author.

d. Notice the *atmosphere* or mood. Sorrow and agony pervade Jesus' experience in Gethsemane. Galatians 1 radiates the heat of Paul's anger toward the Judaizers and his perplexity over the Galatians. Psalm 100 is filled with joy. While this is a more subjective aspect of Bible study, it can give you rich insights into what the author or characters are feeling.

5. Compare Your Interpretation with a Good Commentary

Once you feel you have understood the main subject of the passage and what the author is saying about it, compare your interpretation with that of a good commentary. It can give you additional insights that you might have missed. It can also serve as a corrective if you have misunderstood something the author has said. The *New Bible Commentary* is an excellent one-volume commentary that will provide help and insight when you need it. But do your best to understand the passage on your own before consulting a commentary.

APPENDIX B

A Sample Study

Here is the complete text of the sample study from *God's Word* for your reference, so you can see how the pieces fit together.

Longing for Christ

John 1:1–5, 14–18

God's Word is alive. We experience the power of the living Word when we read Scripture and are moved to follow its teachings or when we study the Bible with others and discover new truths about faith. And when we are able to encourage others through the promises of Scripture, or—perhaps most importantly—when the eyes of seekers are opened to see the meaning of the biblical account of Christ's death and resurrection, we experience the living Word.

GROUP DISCUSSION. When and how has Scripture come to life for you?

PERSONAL REFLECTION. Spend some time thanking God for what he has taught you from Scripture thus far.

John 1 describes how the Word (God's message to the people of planet earth) was revealed to us in Christ. *Read John 1:1–5, 14–18.*

1. What do we learn about the Word in these verses?
2. What do God's actions in these verses reveal about his character?
3. How do you respond to this picture of Christ as the Word?
4. Why do you think the name "the Word" is used here?
5. Why is the role of the Word in creation emphasized so strongly (vv. 1–4)?
6. In what ways do people today fail to see the light shining through the darkness?
7. What do you find significant about the fact that the Word became flesh (v. 14)?
8. What are some ways that we see God's glory?
9. How can we, like John (v. 15), declare Christ's glory to others?
10. How is the law a precursor to Jesus, the Word?
11. We read in four different verses that the Word was with God. Why is this point emphasized?
12. How can regarding Scripture as God's living Word impact the way you handle it?

Ask God to be with you as you continue to study his Word and to impress his truth on your heart.

Now or Later

Read these verses in a couple different Bible versions, especially a paraphrase like *The Message* or the New Living Translation. Note the words or images that stand out. How is your understanding of this passage deepened or expanded?

Resources

<www.ivpress.com/smallgroups> Visit the IVP website's small group area and check out the idea center for resources on community, outreach, worship and prayer, and nurture. You may also sign up for our online newsletter *Small Talk*.

<www.amazon.co.uk> All of IVP's Bible studies are available in Amazon's Bible study store.

<http://smallgroups.com> The website of Small Group Network is a rich resource for small group leaders and pastors. Member surveys offer help in understanding trends in small group ministry.

Applying the Bible by Jack Kuhatschek (Grand Rapids, Mich.: Zondervan, 1996) goes in-depth into the topic of how we apply the Bible to our lives in a way that is both accurate and edifying.

The Bible 101 series edited by Bill Donahue (Downers Grove, Ill.: InterVarsity Press, 2000) is a series of eight different guides of curriculum for learning good Bible study methods.

Biblical Foundations for Small Group Ministry by Gareth Icenogle (Downers Grove, Ill.: InterVarsity Press, 1994) provides a scriptural and theological context for the place of small groups in Christian life.

Small Group Starter Kit by Jeffrey Arnold (Downers Grove, Ill.: InterVarsity Press, 1995) is a great overview of what small groups are and how to lead one. A helpful appendix offers curriculum for training leaders as well.

Transforming Bible Study by Bob Grahmann (Downers Grove, Ill.: InterVarsity Press, 2003) provides a model for doing excellent and engaging Bible study in a postmodern culture.